W9-AGB-470

SUPERSTARS OF FILM

sharon stone

David Sandison

CHELSEA HOUSE PUBLISHERS
Philadelphia

First published in traditional hardback edition
© 1998 by Chelsea House Publishers.
Printed in Hong Kong
Copyright © Parragon Book Service Ltd 1995
Unit 13–17, Avonbridge Trading Estate, Atlantic Road
Avonmouth, Bristol, England BS11 9QD

Library of Congress Cataloging-in-Publication Data
Sandison, David.
    Sharon Stone / by David Sandison.
        p.   cm. — (Superstars of film)
    Originally published: London : Parragon Books, 1996.
    Filmography: p.
    Includes index.
    Summary: A biography of the actress who had driven herself
through ten years of bit parts and often demeaning roles
before arriving at the pinnacle of Hollywood superstardom.
    ISBN 0-7910-4650-8 (hardcover)
    1. Stone, Sharon—Juvenil literature. 2. Motion picture actors
and actresses—United States—Biography—Juvenile literature.
[1. Actors and actresses.]   I. Title.   II. Series.
PN2287.S755S25   1997
791.43'028'092—DC21
    [B]   97-22647
                                                                          CIP
                                                                          AC

ACKNOWLEDGMENTS
Aquarius
Cannon (courtesy Kobal)
Carolco (courtesy Kobal)
Carolco/TriStar (courtesy Kobal)
Kobal Collection
Paramount (courtesy Kobal)
TriStar (courtesy Kobal)
Warner Bros. (courtesy Kobal)
Yog Prods (courtesy Kobal)

CONTENTS

Sharon Stone in Casino

The emotion was real, no doubt about it. As Sharon Stone stood in the spotlight at the Golden Globe Awards in January 1996, her voice breaking with emotion, she clutched the trophy that confirmed her victory in the Best Actress category—deservedly won for her excellent performance in the Martin Scorsese film *Casino*—and fought to deliver the traditional list of thanks to everyone who'd helped make that triumph possible.

One name missing from the roll call she blurted out at the Beverly Hilton event was her own. If there is any one person who should take full credit for her arrival at the pinnacle of Hollywood superstardom, it is Sharon Stone herself. She had driven herself through ten years of bit parts and often demeaning roles in an almost unbroken run of turkeys and disasters to reach the point where she'd become one of the world's highest-paid female movie stars.

Superstardom had been achieved, in one bold stroke, by her performance as the sexually ambidextrous and ferociously promiscuous Catherine Tramell in the 1991 thriller *Basic Instinct*. The scenes with leading man Michael Douglas pushed back the boundaries way beyond anything an establishment studio had dared show before. Perhaps even more importantly, those years of dues-paying, watching, and learning had produced an actress who had finally been able to prove that she was much more than a very beautiful face and a glorious body. America's film and TV critics—the very tough constituency responsible for nominating and selecting recipients for Golden Globe Awards—had recognized that by giving her a prize that confirmed her status and her legitimacy, they had made her an almost automatic choice for an Oscar nomination.

Sharon Stone's tears probably owed much to the fact that she had been recognized as a legitimate actress, for there were still many people only too ready to confuse the real-life actress with the suggestive roles she played. Like many other Hollywood stars, she also had to face the more harmful slurs of Hollywood's notoriously harsh rumor mill, which claimed that many of them had used the proverbial casting couch to secure many early roles.

Sharon's dignity in the face of such scandalous accusations was impressive. There was perhaps some comfort in knowing that such allegations only fly when lesser, jealous people are looking to score sleazy points from those who've proved successful—which only confirmed that Sharon Stone really had succeeded in reaching the top.

Her arrival at the top was assured at the 1995 Cannes Film Festival, when the giant Miramax Films company announced that it had signed Sharon to a $50 million deal that would give her the freedom to produce or star in a string of major projects. In one stroke she became a leading player in the world's biggest and richest game. At the age of thirty-six, Sharon Stone had finally won the right to call all the shots and steer her own course through the film world's shark-infested waters. She at last had the chance to be her own woman.

Sharon Stone at Cannes

Sharon Stone in her modeling years

MEADVILLE TO NEW YORK

About thirty-six miles south of the Great Lakes city of Erie, just off Interstate 79, lies the small West Pennsylvania steel town of Meadville (population 15,000). Sharon Stone was born in this little town on March 10, 1958, and soon after began making a definite impression. The second of four children born to Joseph and Dorothy Stone, she could walk and talk at only ten months and started her formal education, at the age of five, by being bumped immediately into the second grade.

Recalling that time, Sharon has described herself as "a very intense, weird kid." She had, she said, "adult questions and wanted adult answers." A series of tests would give her bewildered parents and beleaguered teachers the answer they sought: little Sharon Stone was precociously and prodigiously intelligent, with an IQ of 154. "I was like a forty-year-old at birth, very intense," she laughs. "My mother just used to look at me in a horrified way!"

In a town like Meadville such precocity is guaranteed to create a canyon of mistrust, even ostracism. Enforced solitude didn't worry Sharon too much—she was too locked into absorbing all the information she could find. While her peers did the usual things kids do during school breaks, she'd find a quiet corner and read. At home she was, she claims, "a nerdy ugly duckling who sat in the back of the closet with a flashlight" to continue her self-education.

To the delight of her father, an engineer with his own small tool and die company, Sharon also displayed an early aptitude for all things technical, especially math and science. Although he tried to interest her in an engineering career, his daughter, now in her teens, had begun to experience the thrill of dressing up and performing, initially in the small world of the family garage and later in school productions. While Sharon's acting in those shows was capable, none of her teachers or peers can recall anything to suggest they were in the presence of one of Hollywood's biggest future stars. The truth was that academic pursuits continued to play by far the greater part in the youngster's life. Selected for a MENSA experiment with gifted children, she would spend half of each school day at Edinboro State College working alongside much older students, as well as taking on more advanced course work in her Saegertown High School classes.

It is perhaps typical of Sharon that the subjects she found herself able to absorb easily began to be put on the back burner, while the more challenging areas of art and architecture—topics that demanded imagination and interpretation—began to take up more of her time and enthusiasm. Interestingly, she claims to have taken up acting at school mainly because it was something she wasn't particularly good at—it was a challenge. She began to haunt Meadville's only movie theater, and old school friends have very clear memories of Sharon announcing that she would one day be "the new Marilyn Monroe." By her midteens, that prediction didn't seem too ridiculous. The "weird nerd" had grown into a very lovely young girl, albeit one who wore a lot of make-up and tried many hair dyes in a bid to counterbalance her reputation as an intellectual.

It is probably no coincidence that boys had begun to play an increasingly active role in Sharon Stone's hectic schedule, but the two main loves of her teenage life were doomed to

Andrew McCarthy and Sharon in Year of the Gun

die violently. First was Craig Grindell, the son of a wealthy family who owned several local factories. A handsome daredevil, and proud owner of an expensive Corvette sports car, Grindell died one night when he and a group of friends raced their cars on a country road. Determined to prove his machine could outpace anything, he was doing 100 mph when his Corvette hit a concrete post and exploded in flames. Sharon was devastated when told of Craig's death, and friends still believe that if he hadn't been killed, the two would have married and Sharon would probably have stayed in Meadville.

Time eventually heals, however, and Sharon became the regular companion of Ray Butterfield, a school football star. Ray and Sharon were the American Teen Dream personified, beau and belle of the high school prom, spending hours at the Butterfield house listening to music and talking, or cruising around the countryside on Ray's motorcycle. But the dream turned into nightmare when Ray was killed one evening while riding to Sharon's house. No one was ever able to explain why or how his bike went out of control on a road he knew well, but it was another terrible tragedy for Sharon, and another episode for amateur psychologists to cite in their attempts to explain her apparent inability to maintain long-relationships in later years.

Sharon also had her own personal brush with death in 1974, when her car hit a patch of ice and crashed. Thrown from the wreck, Sharon narrowly missed smashing into a tree, which undoubtedly would have killed her. That accident had nothing to do with the long scar she has on her neck to this day, but everything to do with a clothesline that caught her across the throat while she was horseback riding and dumped her unceremoniously, and unconscious, to the ground.

Sharon's departure from Meadville eventually came not from the anticipated route of a glittering college life, but from victory in the local Miss Crawford County beauty contest. Sharon still claims someone else entered her, but her old friends are sure she initiated her appearance herself. As Miss Crawford County, Sharon automatically qualified for a place in the Miss Pennsylvania pageant in Philadelphia. It was Sharon's first taste of big city glamour and, in her version of events, the first time she'd even ridden in an elevator. Although she didn't win the Miss Pennsylvania contest, one of the judges suggested to her mother that Sharon should head for New York and try for a modeling career.

Although she was by then involved in a relationship with Richard Baker, Jr., the son of her high school principal, Sharon seized on the idea enthusiastically. She'd been shown an escape route from Meadville and was determined to take it. During the Christmas and New Year holiday of 1976–77, Sharon and her mother stayed in New York, aiming to score an audition with the influential Eileen Ford Model Agency. Dorothy Stone advised caution, pointing out that Sharon could always return to Meadville and her studies if the modeling world didn't want her.

Sharon wasn't listening, and Sharon was right. At the age of eighteen she was signed up by Eileen Ford, returned to Meadville only to pack and say goodbye to Richard Baker, and headed back to New York to begin what would become a three-year career as a successful international runway model.

Sharon in action with Schwarzenegger in Total Recall

DIETS AND DAYDREAMS

If the film world has any real parallel it must be that of high-fashion modeling. Both demand and produce a remarkable degree of narcissism in those who aspire to stardom. Both inflict immense strains on those who achieve success or who are desperate to retain it. Physical perfection is a prerequisite because the camera has a terrible tendency to seek, find, and magnify any flaws. If you are, as Sharon has laughingly described herself, "the fattest thin girl I know," the battle to achieve the ultra-slim, almost androgynous ideal that most designers demand can be particularly brutal. Regular diets are often not enough and after that the liberal and constant use of quack medications becomes the desperate las resort.

Sharon nearly became a victim of this system in her early days as a model. The woman who calls herself "a big farm girl" found herself existing on a diet of little more than crackers and water. Leaving the relative safety of the Ford Agency's dormitory accommodation, and acting on someone's recommendation, she became a patient of a Manhattan "specialist" who claimed to have a completely safe treatment guaranteed to burn away any excess fat on her already slender frame. Daily injections did seem to do the trick, but they also left Sharon desperately ill, dizzy, and weak. One day she was so ill—shaking uncontrollably and with a thundering headache—that friends had to rush her to a genuine doctor's office. Unwilling to admit that she was inflicting the so-called "hormone treatment" on herself, Sharon returned home to endure the effects of self-imposed withdrawal from what she later learned was a horrifying cocktail of pregnant women's urine and sheep embryos!

Others were not so fortunate and a lot of the girls she worked with became habitual drug users, then addicts, before dying. "The late seventies and early eighties were a very decadent time," Sharon has said. "People were free-basing cocaine, partying all night long and having wild sex. I wasn't into that—I'd go to the clubs all night, but drink mineral water. It was like working out to me."

While others seemed determined to burn themselves out, Sharon's Pennsylvania upbringing kept her feet firmly on the ground. As others blew their substantial earnings on fast times, she invested prudently in pension schemes and savings accounts. As one of the Ford Agency's top models she found herself jetting to Paris, London, South Africa, Japan, and Italy, and these savings soon became a substantial safety net that she knew she'd need when her runway days were over and she pitched herself into the even more precarious world of acting.

Looking to the future, Sharon also invested in a succession of drama courses. Her work as a model was, she remembers, "a good gig. I can get it up and look good, but being in that world always seemed like such a scam to me. I was always uncomfortable, but at the same time I was able to make great money so that I didn't have to be a starving artist while I studied acting and lost my Pennsylvania accent." That "good gig" would stand her in fine stead in 1995, when she joined the likes of Naomi Campbell, Cindy Crawford, Kate Moss, and Linda Evangelista in *Unzipped,* a behind-the-scenes documentary about the rarified environment of modeling, directed by Robert Leacock.

By 1980 Sharon Stone was back in New York and, while

still pursuing her modeling career, had begun studying method acting. She also began turning out for auditions, soon learning that she was only one of thousands of other beautiful young men and women desperate to "get into movies." It looked like it might be a very long haul unless she had a vital stroke of luck.

Cue "Lucky Break" music. Enter Woody Allen, stage left. Lights, camera, action!

With Sylvester Stallone in The Specialist

WELCOME TO TINSELTOWN

In 1980 Woody Allen made *Stardust Memories,* a darkly comedic film about a comedy filmmaker trying to fend off attacks for making serious films. In homage to his idol, Ingmar Bergman, Allen peppered the movie with surreal Bergmanesque sequences, including one in which Allen's character, Sandy Bates, finds himself trapped in a stationary train filled with glum, vacant-faced people. Across the tracks a train full of laughing, happy characters stands tantalizingly but unattainably close. Worse, as that train pulls away, a beautiful and sexy girl looks directly at Sandy and mouths a lascivious kiss.

"For this scene I needed someone who would look startling, but not comic book," Allen has recalled. "I wanted a real fantasy woman. We must have looked at and talked to scores of girls, but Sharon was the one. I looked at her and thought I'd really like her to kiss me!" Sharon was given the job of providing that brief but memorable image that Allen hoped would disturb and stay with his audience. "You take a chance on a moment and a person and hope it works," Allen explained. "This one did, quite wonderfully."

Although uncredited in *Stardust Memories,* Sharon Stone had impressed herself on the movie world, and she decided to go for broke and move to Los Angeles. Living in a small apartment in Beverly Hills, Sharon began the slow march around production offices and agencies. Keenly aware of her shortcomings, she joined a number of acting workshops, attended dance and voice classes, and began studying privately with drama coach Roy London, a man she credits with being her best teacher and whose death from AIDS in 1994 was a blow from which many say she has yet to recover.

Given Sharon's stunning looks and modeling-based poise and elegance, it was no surprise that she soon found herself in demand as a guest at the never-ending round of Hollywood parties, where unflawed beauty is the minimum requirement for entry. Most of the more vicious rumors about Sharon date from this period, and while it's undeniably true that not all the lovelies who rub shoulders (and more) with the movie world's most powerful and influential people are there to pursue a legitimate acting career, there are scores more whose presence is due to the skills of managers and agents able to get their talented clients into a vital part of the Hollywood business scene.

It's a measure of both Sharon Stone's sense of humor and her forbearance that malicious stories or gossip column items are regularly added to a large heart-shaped bulletin board that she calls "Cupid" and keeps at home for her own amusement. But those stories have hurt, prompting Sharon to one notable outburst: "If you are a woman finding any degree of success, it seems to have escaped the 'minds' in this environment that you could have possibly earned it by professionalism and integrity. That you [slept] your way to the top seems a more palatable concept."

She doesn't deny that there were times when she found herself subjected to casting couch moves, though she chooses to recount them wittily. "The first time I turned down a studio executive who wanted to sleep with me, he screamed: 'You'll never work in this town again!' I thought that was the funniest thing I'd ever heard. When a well-known producer opened his zipper . . . during a meeting, I thought it was the funniest thing I'd ever seen!" The trouble with Sharon Stone—and a fact she is now prepared to admit—was that while she may have been blessed, or cursed, with stunning looks, she was also much smarter than the average Hollywood executive.

All the study, the workouts, and the endless parties paid off in 1981 when Sharon found herself on the way to Texas for her first real screen role—as one of three girls in a remote farmhouse who find themselves up against a religious sect and a mysterious, murderous intruder. *Deadly Blessing* would prove to be only the first time she'd be asked to appear in what she rightly calls "knucklehead B-movies where you have to play every character as a drug addict or an alcoholic and there would be no explanation for it."

This particular "knucklehead" outing was directed by Wes Craven, still three years away from the fame and fortune of *Nightmare on Elm Street,* but this time working with a miniscule budget, laughable script, and effects that were less than special. But at least it enabled Sharon to meet and befriend Craven's then-wife, Mimi, still her closest friend.

The year 1981 also brought a ray of promise in the form of a small part in Claude Lelouche's *Les Unes et Les Autres* (also known as *Bolero*), which gave Sharon the chance to watch the likes of James Caan and Geraldine Chaplin working to overcome the challenges of playing multiple roles in a story that jumped in and out of flashback with confusing regularity.

Back in Hollywood again, Sharon found film work no easier to get. However, many people were making movies and series for television. Work was work, after all, and experience was experience, so she spent almost all of the next three years in a succession of made-for-TV films (including *Not Just Another Affair* and *The Calendar Girl Murders*), as well as popping up in successful series like *Magnum PI* and *Remington Steel.*

In 1983 Sharon learned first-hand that there is no such

thing as a sure-fire, dead-certain project when she was signed up to play the wife of a baseball player for twenty-one episodes of a major new drama series, *Bay City Blues*. Set in and around San Francisco, the show was the brainchild of Steve Bochco, creator of *Hill Street Blues* and *NYPD Blue*. The first three episodes were greeted by overwhelmingly negative critical response and indifferent audience reaction, and *Bay City Blues* was sunk without trace.

But it would be the experience of playing opposite Rock Hudson in the 1984 TV movie *The Vegas Strip Wars* that would prove a watershed in Sharon Stone's life, both professionally and personally.

The Quick and the Dead, *the first film Sharon produced*

Sharon described her role in King Solomon's Mines *as "a bad hairdo running through the jungle!"*

ROCK, LOVE, AND JUNGLE NIGHTS

Rock Hudson knew he had full-blown AIDS—and was beginning to show the first signs of the disease—by the time filming began on *The Vegas Strip Wars*, in which he played a casino boss and Sharon Stone was the cigarette girl with whom he has an affair. The two got along extremely well, creating a friendship Sharon continues to treasure a decade after Hudson finally died. His dignity and honesty inspired Elizabeth Taylor to launch her international AIDS charity. Hudson confided in Sharon fully, was incredibly helpful and supportive of her work, and confirmed his affection by promising that he'd act as godfather to the children she and Michael Greenburgh would have. *The Vegas Strip Wars* had also introduced Sharon to a helter-skelter love affair and marriage—in Erie, on August 18, 1984—to Greenburgh, the film's thirty-three-year-old producer. The two set up home in Beverly Hills, Sharon cruising Rodeo Drive in a BMW 325E, Greenburgh zooming to meetings in his Alfa Romeo. They were the ideal Hollywood couple.

Their happiness had been compounded by the release and critical success of *Irreconcilable Differences*. The film starred Shelley Long (the first big-screen outing for this actress from the hit TV sitcom *Cheers*) and Ryan O'Neal, whose daughter (played by ten-year-old Drew Barrymore) tries to sue her parents for divorce. Sharon played a waitress with whom O'Neal, a film director, is besotted. Her playing of the part—a rare and treasured chance for her to show off her comedic skills—brought rave reviews, one of which opined: "Sharon Stone steals the movie from Shelley Long and O'Neal."

The dream marriage turned sour and ended in separation and divorce only twenty-six months later—pushed toward breakup by the strain of spending most of 1985 filming in Africa, for *King Solomon's Mines* and *Allan Quartermain and the Lost City of Gold*. The brainchild of the Cannon Group moguls Manahem Golan and Yoram Globus, both films starred former Dr. Kildare heartthrob Richard Chamberlain and were designed to cash in on the adventure thriller boom started by Steven Spielberg's *Indiana Jones* movies. Both were to be filmed entirely on location in Zimbabwe, with J. Lee-Thompson directing the former and Gary Nelson the latter. Michael Greenburgh was given the task of looking after Cannon's interests for the second.

Everything that could go wrong did, calamitously and disastrously. Zimbabwe—three years into a drought everyone said would last another year—turned into a swamp as the rains finally came, then stayed. The country was in the middle of a buildup to bitterly fought elections that meant locations were often under armed guard as army patrols kept a wary lookout for rebel forces. Worse, all versions of the scripts were terrible, leading Sharon laughingly to summarize her contribution to *King Solomon's Mines* and *Allan Quartermain* as "a bad hairdo running through the jungle!"

It was a nightmare. "Making those films was incredibly destructive to my marriage," Sharon would recall later. "We were both locked into making horrible movies for people who didn't [care] what we were doing anyway. I was

Sharon and Steven Segal in Above the Law

panic-stricken because I was months in Africa making movies I knew were destroying my career. I was constantly trying to push and provoke everybody to make them good movies. My marriage was falling apart, the movies were going to be bad," she conceded.

After the African fiasco, with her marriage on the rocks and her year away from the Hollywood action causing everyone to ask, "Sharon Who?" she began accepting almost any film role she was offered—more dumb bimbo or terrorized victim roles. One day she simply took stock of where she was and what she was doing, and decided the time had come to take more control.

Sharon made a complete break by accepting a role in *Police Academy 4: Citizens on Patrol,* the last in a series of broad comedies that never garnered good reviews but consistently became big box-office successes. Working with Steve Guttenburg and eleven other stand-up comedians was, Sharon says, "a wonderful antidote to that year in Africa."

Now represented by top manager Chuck Binder, Sharon was encouraged to go for bigger and better roles, and although she failed to win the part played by Glenn Close in *Fatal Attraction,* or that of journalist Vicki Vale in *Batman* (it went to Kim Basinger), or the sexy Breathless Mahoney in *Dick Tracy* (a role given to Madonna), Binder was at least pitching her at the right level. It began to pay off.

During 1987 she made the thriller *Cold Steel* and then won the lead female role in the TV movie *Tears in the Rain,* a weepy World War II romance that saw her and Christopher Cazenove spark nicely off each other, even if reviewers didn't think much of it. The following year she was back in harassed female mode for the thrillers *Action Jackson* and *Above the Law,* the latter a brutal vehicle for Steven Seagal, a former martial arts expert attempting to join Stallone and Schwarzenegger as a big-screen action star. She was also able to add to her growing experience with good performances in a Spanish remake of the 1941 Rita Hayworth film

Blood and Sand (Sangre y Arena) and the Martin Sheen movie *Beyond the Stars,* in which her warmth and sensitivity helped soothe the fevered brow of his veteran astronaut character. The critics, however, remained unsure.

But Sharon's stock was to rise immeasurably in 1989 with the release of the blockbuster TV mini-series *War and Remembrance,* in which she received a major credit and critical acclaim. Filmed over a three-year period at a cost of $110 million, it was a sequel to the highly successful *The Winds of War.* Like its predecessor, it starred Robert Mitchum and a host of big international "names"—including Sir John Gielgud, Victoria Tennant, Jane Seymour, Robert Hardy, Barbara Steele, and Ralph Bellamy.

Total Recall *with Arnold Schwarzenegger:*
"The fight scenes with Arnold were exhausting,
but they were a blast."

ARNIE, *PLAYBOY,* AND MICHAEL

If there was anything Sharon Stone was not looking for in 1989, it was another action movie. When she was first approached for *Total Recall,* a sci-fi epic that was to star Arnold Schwarzenegger, the Austrian-born bodybuilder who'd miraculously transformed himself into one of the world's most popular film stars, her first reaction was to reply, Thanks, but no thanks! What stopped her was the fact that *Total Recall* was to be directed by Paul Verhoeven, the Dutch filmmaker whose early adventurous pre-Hollywood work Sharon had long admired. Since taking up residence in the States he'd had a huge hit with *Robocop,* the excellence of which had also attracted Schwarzenegger. If it was good enough for Verhoeven, Sharon surmised, *Total Recall* had to be good enough for her.

A look at the script showed that, for once, her character was not going to be another decorative victim. Before being shot by Arnie's character, Quaid, Sharon was going to get the opportunity to force him to dive for cover under a hail of bullets, cut him across the chest with a kitchen knife, and hit him where it hurts most with her fist and foot. In order to make her (temporary) defeat of the former Mr. Universe even remotely feasible, Sharon embarked on an exhaustive two-month bodybuilding and fitness course. This entailed circuit training, karate, a succession of weight machines, then sit-ups and stretching exercises. Then, during the twenty weeks of filming in Mexico City, she worked out in the hotel gymnasium.

"I worked my buns off," she recounts. "I'd work out until guys would puke, and only then I'd stop. But before it was over, I was big, I was buff, I could kick some butt! The fight scenes with Arnold were exhausting, but they were a blast." She also got to be manipulatively sexy, though Paul Verhoeven's direction ensured that while the brief bedroom scene between the two was erotically charged, Sharon got to keep her nightdress on.

When it was released in 1990, *Total Recall* completely obliterated rivals like *Dick Tracy* at the international box office, made Arnold Schwarzenegger an estimated $30 million (his cut of global profits in addition to his $10 million fee), and focused attention on Sharon Stone as never before. It seemed that nothing could go wrong now, but the fates decreed otherwise. Just after finishing work on *Total Recall*, Sharon was driving home from a Roy London acting class when her BMW was hit by a Cadillac being driven on the wrong side of the road. In deep shock, Sharon sat on the street, unrecognized and untreated, for three hours. In fact, she had suffered a severe concussion, a dislocated jaw, a broken rib, a sprained back, and a badly twisted knee.

At precisely the time when she ought to have been able to use the success of *Total Recall* to call the shots, Sharon found herself undergoing months of intense physical therapy, her back in a brace and her neck supported by a collar. She also found out who her real friends were, and it was a bitter learning experience. "Some of them who I thought would be wonderful didn't want to know once I was off the scene," Sharon remembers. "I realized I was one of those 'life of the party' girls—once I was in bed with a broken body and couldn't be entertaining, they weren't around any more. So those 'friends' were given a big clear-out." The hard work she'd put into getting herself in shape for *Total Recall* left

Sharon in excellent condition to speed her recovery and confound the doctors who delivered gloomy prognoses about her long-term mobility. To prove them wrong, and to confound everyone else, she also agreed to pose, wearing not much more than a knowing smile, for *Playboy.*

The ten-page feature (entitled "She's Got Hollywood Breathing Heavy") published in the July 1990 issue proved that Sharon Stone—by *Playboy* standards a relatively ancient thirty-two-year-old—had no reason to worry about comparison with the magazine's more usual airbrushed Barbies. Here was a very self-assured, very beautiful, and very sexy mature woman. She defends the *Playboy* session by saying she wanted to make a statement against the popular misconception that thirty-something women somehow lose their sex appeal. "I don't give a damn about age," she says. "I earned every single one of my years." There was also the large amount of money *Playboy* paid her, which she cheerfully admits did wonders for reducing the mortgage she'd just taken out on a new house.

Later in 1990 Sharon relocated to Rome for filming of *Year of the Gun,* a political thriller directed by John Frankenheimer. The next few months were a blur of nonstop activity, though not always to any great artistic end. But Sharon was working hard and 1991 saw the release of three more movies—*Scissors, He Said, She Said,* and *Diary of a Hitman,* which finally gave her the welcome chance to work under the direction of her dramatic guru, Roy London.

And, of course, there was *Basic Instinct,* a film in which Sharon Stone, Michael Douglas, and Paul Verhoeven got to rewrite the rules about what was—and what was not—permissible in depicting sex on the big screen. It also confirmed the arrival, after ten long years, of Sharon Stone as a 24-carat movie star.

Sharon as Catherine Tramell in Basic Instinct

A BASIC INSTINCT TO WIN

The part of Catherine Tramell—the ice-cool, bisexual thriller writer who becomes chief suspect in the hunt for a Black Widow killer—had been offered to a number of other better-known and more established actresses (most notably leading man Michael Douglas's personal first choice, Isabelle Adjani) before Sharon Stone was asked if she'd like to try out for it. She had two reasons for instantly agreeing. First, the sex scenes were going to be astonishingly frank, but they were to be enacted by a powerful, smart, seductive woman. It was a challenging role she knew she could handle, and handle superbly if she was given the chance. Second, the film was already notorious in America, having been bought at auction from screenwriter Joe Eszterhas for a record $3 million. "I read the script and thought, Oh, man, some-body's going to be so good in this!" Sharon has said. "I never got why everybody didn't just die for the part. I guess a lot of people had more to lose than I did."

Basic Instinct fascinated Hollywood watchers, largely due to the chemistry between Douglas and Stone, as well as the sultry scenes where only Sharon is on film. In one of these scenes, her character, Catherine Trammell, is in a interroga-tion room at the police station and slyly diverts the attention away from her culpability by seductively crossing and uncrossing her legs. Her trick works and the actors in the film and the people in the theatres realize that Sharon Stone can distract and charm both the audience and the camera.

That moment, along with the rest of the controversy surrounding *Basic Instinct*—including gay rights protests against the sterotypical depiction of a bisexual woman as a murderous predator, and Christian fundamentalists condemnation of the film—would guarantee even greater box office returns and inevitably, even greater fame for Stone.

Which, of course, it did. Sharon Stone became a very hot property thanks to *Basic Instinct,* raised her fee to a reputed $6 million per movie, and was able to take her pick of offers that began flooding in. Her first project was *Sliver,* a messy tangle about voyeurism and murder. Although it did incredibly well when released (pulling in an estimated $78 million in theaters worldwide and becoming the most-rented video in the United States in 1993), it was something of an ordeal to make.

Although it boasted another Joe Eszterhas script, *Sliver* cast Sharon opposite William Baldwin, an actor she couldn't warm to, in a story that threw her back into the old territory of threatened victim, even if that victim was supposed to be a top publishing editor. Five different endings were shot, and the sex scenes with Baldwin in the film were embarrassingly bad.

Her parents have been consistently supportive of Sharon's steamier roles, refusing to criticize her exposure in films like *Basic Instinct* or revealing photo sessions in magazines like *Playboy,* or admit to any embarrassment. Her father has been quoted as saying, "We all do it, right? It didn't embarrass me any. I thought she looked beautiful in the magazine, and if it helped her career, why not? She asked for my approval—I gave it happily."

It was during the making of *Sliver* that Sharon's private life went ballistically public. She began an affair with Bill MacDonald, a married associate of Robert Evans, the film's producer, breaking off a long-standing relationship with

With Michael Douglas in Basic Instinct

Chris Peters, the twenty-four-year-old son of Hollywood tycoon Jon Peters. Sharon set up house with MacDonald and announced their engagement in a 1993 Oscars night TV talk show hosted by Barbara Walters. MacDonald's wife, Naomi, went on the offensive with a series of interviews that cast Sharon as a predatory woman who'd caused her to miscarry. Her story lost some of its tragic edge when she and Joe Eszterhas (another married man) began an affair that ended his marriage. Meanwhile, Bill's mother got in on the act by telling a U.S. tabloid: "Sharon's a slut. . . . She's a bad person." Another clipping for the "Cupid" board.

Sharon then went to Vancouver—to play Richard Gere's wife in the film *Intersection,* a movie she says Paramount ruined by re-editing—and met and fell for Frank Anderson, a Canadian stockbroker she'd literally pursued when their cars drew alongside each other at a traffic light. Despite extreme caution on their part, rumors began to spread. Exit Anderson and, shortly afterward, exit MacDonald. The new man in her life (for a while at least) was to be Bob Wagner, the son of actor Robert. More rumors have linked her variously with Revlon cosmetics owner Ron Perelman, country music superstar Dwight Yoakam, Warren Beatty, and Jack Nicholson.

Sharon's next venture was *The Quick and the Dead,* a Western that was to be her first movie as producer. Costarring Gene Hackman, *The Quick and the Dead* enabled her to give her older brother, Michael, a role as Hackman's largely mute sidekick. A one-time drug dealer who'd spent two years in prison for possessing cocaine in the seventies, Michael had rehabilitated himself with Sharon's help, and he'd set up business in Los Angeles and married Rona Newton-John, sister of Olivia.

The Quick and the Dead fared moderately well at the box office, but scored a public-relations triumph when it was chosen to close the 1995 Cannes Film Festival. French cinema buffs greeted her arrival for the screening with hysteria. The

With Richard Gere in *Intersection*

country's love affair with Sharon was cemented later in the year when the Minister of Culture bestowed on her the prestigious title of Chevalier dans l'Ordre des Arts et des Lettres for her services to the performing arts.

Then it was off to Miami to begin filming *The Specialist* with Sylvester Stallone, a thriller with spectacular explosions and a couple of steamy sex scenes that seemed calculated to prove that the Stallone pecs were still in great shape. It was obvious that Sharon's were, too. This time the sex scenes were shot behind closed doors with a minimal crew subject to confidentiality agreements. This was initiated by Stallone, not Sharon Stone.

In box-office terms, *The Specialist* was dynamite, even if movie critics sniffed. More importantly, perhaps, Stallone went to great lengths to help dispel his costar's growing reputation as a "difficult" person by telling reporters that it had been the smoothest-run set of his career: "There have been no difficulties, no prima donnas. Sharon? A delight."

In five short years, Sharon Stone had played opposite three of the world's biggest male superstars (Schwarzenegger, Douglas, and Stallone) and worked with two of the most accomplished screen actors (Gere and Hackman). She now set her sights on working with someone who was not only one of the biggest but was also arguably the best—Robert De Niro.

Sharon in The Specialist

Sharon was awed to be working with Robert De Niro in Casino

WELCOME TO THE CASINO

Sharon Stone was initially reluctant to put herself forward for the part of Ginger McKenna—the cocktail waitress and call girl wooed and married by a Mafia boss played by Robert De Niro—whose increasingly outrageous behavior makes her a dangerous liability and eventually threatens the crime syndicate's Las Vegas empire. The fact that *Casino* was to be directed by Martin Scorsese, had been written by Nicholas Pileggi (the coauthor of Scorsese's hit movie *GoodFellas*), and would also costar such powerful actors as Joe Pesci and James Woods (who'd played the sadist who manipulated her character in *The Specialist*), was enough to make even the most self-assured actress hesitate. Despite her undoubted success, Sharon Stone is still refreshingly uncertain about her acting skills.

Unbelievably, she was asked to audition for *Casino,* an ordeal she hates and admits to rarely doing well. Even when it was confirmed that she'd won the part, the doubts remained. "If I get up to bat with them and I just stink, then what?" she admitted later. "Then what do you tell yourself? Time to move to a new town and get a new job?"

The full realization of the challenge came, she says, on the very first scene she was due to shoot opposite De Niro. The two had met on a number of occasions over the years and had become what she calls "amicable acquaintances."

She'd come to know and like "Bob" De Niro, but the moment the set fell silent and Martin Scorsese called "Action!" she looked across the table "and found myself looking at Robert De Niro . . . I mean, Robert De Niro!" But De Niro, Scorsese and Pesci became an ad hoc cheerleading section, urging Sharon to let it all hang out. "They were like, give it all to us, baby, just let her rip—if you've got it, we want it, let's see what you can do!" she recalls.

Sharon did give it all and prove that she had it. Her performance in *Casino* was exceptional, allowing her to tear through the film like a wayward rocket, delivering humor, madness, pathos, and outrageous vivacity in equally potent doses. She simply stole the picture, and it was inevitable that the award nominations would follow (although she later lost the Best Actress Academy Award to Susan Sarandon for *Dead Man Walking*).

For Sharon, *Casino* was "deeply gratifying in two ways. One, because I see the film and realize it's true—I haven't been deluding myself all these years, I really can do it! That's incredibly gratifying. Then, I got up to bat with my dream people, the one actor I strived all my career to work with—that was the apex. And then there was Marty Scorsese. . . ."

Fame has changed Sharon's life forever. She has been the victim of a stalker, and has been forced to move into a fortress of a house with elaborate security systems. She is accompanied by bodyguards everywhere she goes and her private life has become public property. "The price you pay is no space," she admits. "But good, bad, or indifferent, as long as they're talking, you're still in the game!"

More positively, fame and success have enabled Sharon to create her own all-woman management company—the ironically named Chaos Productions—and to dispense with agents who invariably have their own self-serving axes to grind. These days, with the advice of close and trusted friends (including Mimi Craven, Faye Dunaway, and Roseanne Barr), she makes her own decisions, for better or worse. Fame has also enabled Sharon to give her support and invaluable public relations value to favored charities, including Planet Hope, the charity she and her sister Kelly founded in Los Angeles to help poor and homeless children. She has been known to work there on a voluntary, unpublicized basis.

Sharon has a formidable reputation as a foot-stamper when she thinks her opinions aren't valued or heeded by producers and directors. But that's only fair, her friends say—she's entitled to a deciding vote after fifteen years of being a mere pawn in other people's games. Although the movie establishment continues to view her as something of a maverick, it has recognized her status by giving her a star on Hollywood Boulevard's famous sidewalk.

She recognizes that it could all end tomorrow, but is characteristically accepting of the situation: "I would say there's an enormous possibility that it might happen, although I'd accept the great good fortune of passing it by! But I'm not convinced that any of this is gonna last forever."

Sharon Stone says she has only two long-term ambitions: to shake off her "sex goddess" title and be better known as a fine dramatic actress, and "to do a Jessica Tandy" by stepping up to accept a Best Actress Oscar in her eighties. Given her proven staying power against all odds, it's quite conceivable she could accomplish both.

FILMOGRAPHY

The year refers to the first release date of the film.

1980 *Stardust Memories*
1981 *Deadly Blessing*
1981 *Bolero* (French: *Les Unes et Les Autres*)
1983 *Bay City Blues* (television series)
1984 *Irreconcilable Differences*
1984 *The Vegas Strip Wars* (television movie)
1985 *King Solomon's Mines*
1987 *Allan Quartermain and the Lost City of Gold*
1987 *Police Academy 4: Citizens on Patrol*
1987 *Cold Steel*
1988 *Tears in the Rain* (television movie)
1988 *Action Jackson*
1988 *Above the Law (Nico)*
1989 *Blood and Sand (Spanish: Sangre y Arena)*
1989 *Beyond the Stars (Personal Choice)*
1989 *War and Remembrance* (television miniseries)
1990 *Total Recall*
1991 *Year of the Gun*
1991 *Scissors*
1991 *He Said, She Said*
1991 *Diary of a Hitman*
1991 *Basic Instinct*
1992 *Where Sleeping Dogs Lie*
1993 *Sliver*
1993 *The Last Action Hero*
1994 *The Specialist*
1994 *Intersection*
1995 *The Quick and the Dead*
1995 *Unzipped*
1995 *Casino*
1996 *Last Dance*
1996 *Diabolique*
1997 *Sphere*
1997 *The Mighty*
1998 *Gloria*

INDEX

INDEX

	DATE DUE		

B
Stone, Sharon